FASCINATING SCIENCE PROJECTS

LIGHT

Sally Hewitt

Franklin Watts
London • Sydney

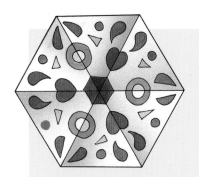

© Aladdin Books Ltd 2002
Produced by
Aladdin Books Ltd
28 Percy Street
London W1T 2BZ

ISBN 0–7496–4495–8

First published in Great Britain in 2002 by
Franklin Watts
96 Leonard Street
London
EC2A 4XD

Designers:
Flick, Book Design & Graphics
Pete Bennett

Editor:
Harriet Brown

Illustrators:
Ian Thompson,
Catherine Ward and Peter Wilks – SGA
Cartoons: Tony Kenyon – BL Kearley

Consultant:
Dr Bryson Gore

Printed in UAE

A CIP catalogue record for this book is available
from the British Library.

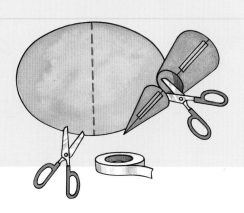

Contents

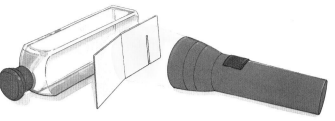

Introduction

In this book, the science of light is explained through a series of fascinating projects and experiments. Each chapter deals with a different topic on light, such as shadows or colours, and contains a major project that is fully supported by simple experiments, 'Magic panels' and 'Fascinating fact' boxes. At the end of every chapter is an explanation of what has happened and what this means. Projects requiring sharp tools or the use of heat should be done with adult supervision.

 **This states the purpose of the project**

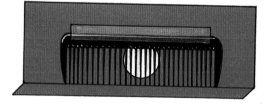 METHOD NOTES
Helpful hints on things to remember when carrying out your project.

Materials
In this box is a full list of the items needed to carry out each main project.

 **Figure 2**

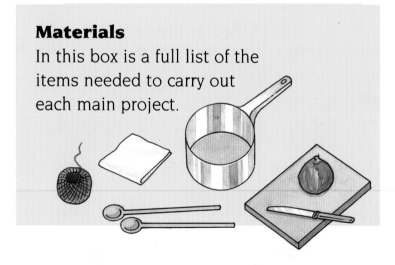

1. The steps that describe how to carry out each project are listed clearly as numbered points.
2. Where there are illustrations to help you understand the instructions, the text refers to them as 'Figure 1', etc.

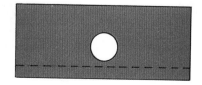 **Figure 1**

4

THE AMAZING MAGIC PANEL
This heading states what is happening

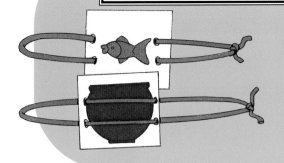

These boxes contain an activity or experiment that has a particularly dramatic or surprising result!

WHY IT WORKS
You can find out exactly what happened here too.

WHY IT WORKS

These boxes, which are headed either 'What this shows' or 'Why it works', contain an explanation of what happened during your project, why it happened and the meaning of the result.

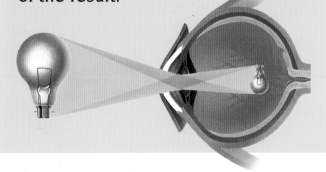

Fascinating facts!
An amusing or surprising fact related to the theme of the chapter.

Where the project involves using a sharp knife, heat or anything else that requires adult supervision, you will see this warning symbol.

The text in these circles links the theme of the topic from one page to the next in the chapter.

What is light?

Light is a kind of energy. We cannot see without it. Light from the Sun lights up Earth by day. At night, when it is dark, we turn on electric lights or light candles to see by. The Sun, electric light bulbs and candles are all luminous, which means they give out light of their own. Light travels very fast in straight lines called rays. When rays of light hit something solid like you, a dark patch called a shadow is formed where the light cannot reach.

Explore how a light bulb glows

METHOD NOTES
Use tweezers to pull out a single wire from soap free steel wool.

Figure 1

Materials
- two 1.5 volt batteries
- 2 pieces of insulated wire
- modelling clay
- 2 crocodile clips
- a single wire from steel wool
- a tray of sand

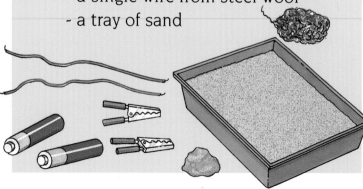

1. Put the two batteries together with a positive (+) terminal touching a negative (-) terminal (Figure 1).
2. Fix the exposed end of one piece of insulated wire to another of the battery terminals using a piece of modelling clay (Figure 1).

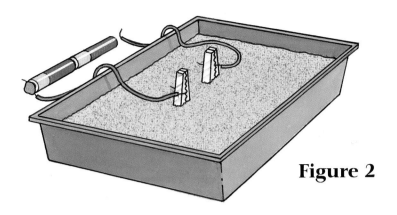

Figure 2

3. Lie the end of the other insulated wire near the remaining battery terminal.
4. Stand the crocodile clips in the sand tray and attach the other ends of the insulated wires to the clips (Figure 2).
5. Attach the single wire from the steel wool between the two crocodile clips (Figure 3).

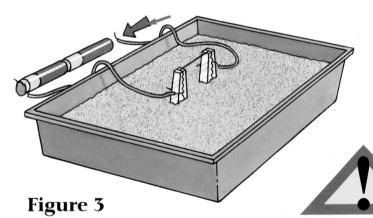

Figure 3

6. Complete the circuit by touching the loose, exposed end of the wire to the battery terminal. Watch the steel wool glow, flare up and break as electricity flows through it (Figure 4). Stand back as the wire flares and don't touch it.

WHAT THIS SHOWS

The steel wool wire makes up part of an electric circuit. It is so thin that it becomes red hot and glows when electricity passes through it.

The wire catches fire and burns out in air. The fine wire in an electric light bulb, called a filament, is made of a metal called tungsten. A light bulb is filled with a gas called argon which lets the filament glow brightly for a long time without burning out.

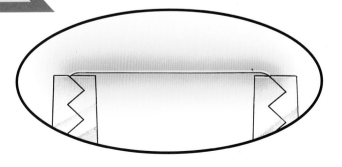

Figure 4

Some luminous things give out brighter light than others. The brightness of light is called intensity. Torchlight is more intense than candlelight. As light spreads out, it becomes less intense.

What is light?

SUNLIGHT AND MOONLIGHT

In a dark room, shine a torch onto a postcard placed inside a box (Figure 1). How well can you see the picture? Make a cone from half a circle of card (Figure 2) and attach it to the end of the torch to direct the beam. Now, crumple a piece of white paper into a ball for the Moon. Stick a length of string to the ball with tape (Figure 3). Hang the ball in front of the box and shine the beam onto the ball to make it glow (Figure 4). How well does the ball light up the picture?

Figure 1

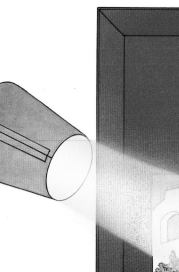

Figure 2

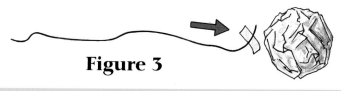

Figure 3

WHAT THIS SHOWS

Sunlight is brighter than moonlight. The Moon has no light of its own. Moonlight is reflected light from the Sun. Torchlight is reflected off the ball of paper. This reflected light is weaker than the light from the torch.

Figure 4

LIGHT AND SHADOW

In a dark room, carefully light a candle and place objects all around it. See how each object around the candle casts a shadow in a different direction.

This happens because a candle spreads light all around it. A beam of torchlight only shines in the direction in which you point it. If you shone a torch at these objects, all the shadows would point away from the torch.

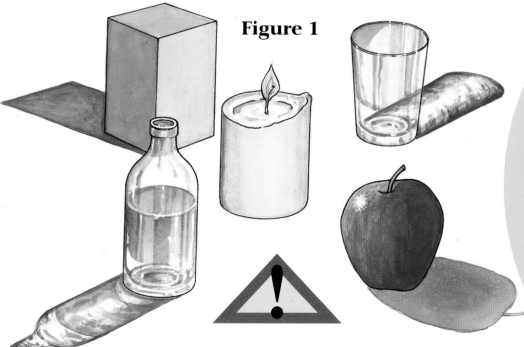

Figure 1

The Sun is the Earth's greatest source of light. We need light to see so we use luminous objects such as electric lights and candles to light up the darkness.

Shadows

When a solid object lies in the path of a ray of light, it creates a dark patch called a shadow where the light cannot reach. Night is created by the Earth's shadow. As the Earth spins around in space, half of it is always facing the Sun and the other half is in shadow. When the part of the Earth that you are on is facing the Sun it is day; when it is facing away from the Sun it is night.

Make a sundial to see how shadows work

METHOD NOTES
Use a compass to position the sundial so that the dowel is on the south edge of the cardboard.

Materials
- modelling clay
- a piece of thick card
- glue
- a length of dowel
- waterproof paints
- a ruler
- a compass

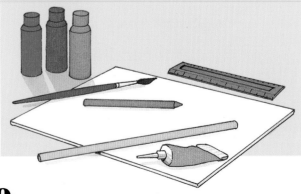

1. Put a piece of modelling clay under the middle of one of the long edges of the card. Push a skewer through the card into the clay to make a hole.

Figure 1

2. Glue the dowel into the hole so that it stands upright (Figure 1).

3. Use waterproof paint to decorate the sundial (Figure 2).

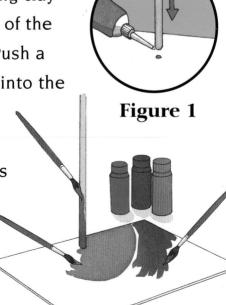

Figure 2

10

4. On a bright sunny morning put the sundial outside. On the hour exactly, draw a line along the shadow made by the dowel and write the time next to it (Figure 3).

5. Repeat this every hour on the hour throughout the day. You will end up with a series of lines on the sundial at even intervals (Figure 4).

6. Use your sundial to tell the time. It will only work on sunny days and if you always place it in exactly the same position.

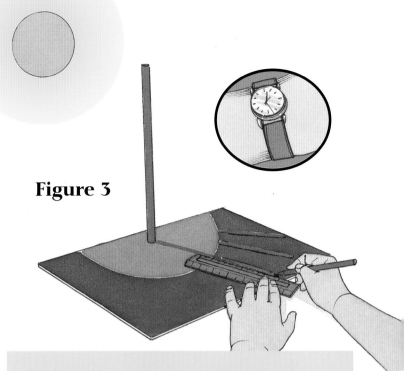

Figure 3

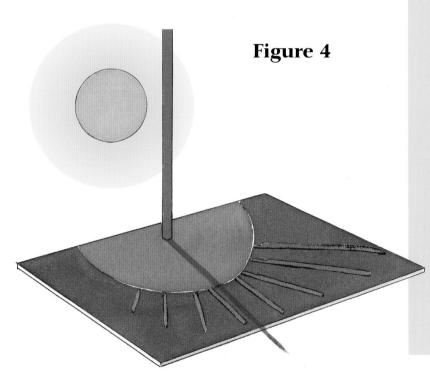

Figure 4

WHAT THIS SHOWS

The dowel casts a shadow where it blocks light from the Sun. The position of the shadow on the sundial changes as the Sun moves across the sky.

In fact, the Sun stays still in space and the Earth revolves around it. To us, it appears that the Sun rises in the east. It reaches its highest point at midday. Then it sets in the west.

Shadows

A small light shone at an object creates a dark shadow called an umbra. When the light is bigger, some light gets around the object, so the edge of the shadow looks grey and is called a penumbra.

HOW SHADOWS CHANGE THROUGHOUT THE DAY

The position of the Sun in the sky affects the length and position of your shadow. On a sunny morning, stand outside on a hard surface.

Get a friend to draw around your shadow with chalk. Stand in the same place at midday and in the afternoon and do the same again. Your shadow is longer in the morning and afternoon when the Sun is low in the sky. It is shorter at midday when the Sun is nearly overhead.

THE AMAZING PUPPET SHOW
Make a puppet show of birds and dogs using your hands

In a dark room, shine a bright torch onto a wall. Copy these shapes with your hands. Put your hands in front of the light and move them to flap wings and wiggle ears.

WHY IT WORKS
Light cannot shine through your hands so a shadow of the shape, or silhouette of your hands, is cast onto the wall. The nearer your hands are to the light, the bigger the shadows will be.

Figure 1

OPAQUE, TRANSLUCENT AND TRANSPARENT

Find a piece of clear plastic, some tissue paper and a piece of card. Shine bright torchlight onto each one in turn. No light will pass through the card and you will see a shadow (Figure 1). Only a little light will pass through the tissue (Figure 2), whereas it will shine right through the clear plastic (Figure 3).

Figure 2

Figure 3

WHY IT WORKS

The card is opaque and lets no light through. The tissue paper is translucent, which means it lets a little light through. The clear plastic is transparent, which means light can shine through it. Clouds are translucent and only let a little sunlight through, so you don't see shadows on a cloudy day.

Light cannot shine through things which are opaque, so opaque things cast a shadow. We can tell the time using a sundial by the changing shadows on a sunny day.

Reflection

As light travels in straight lines it hits objects in its path. It bounces off the objects rather like a ball bouncing off a wall. We see things because light bounces off them. We call this reflection. Rough surfaces scatter light that is reflected in all directions. Smooth, flat surfaces reflect light in one direction. White things show up because white reflects light. Dark colours are hard to see because they absorb or take in light.

Make a kaleidoscope to explore reflected light

METHOD NOTES
If you use mirror board ask an adult to help you cut it with a craft knife.

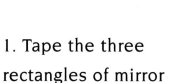

Figure 1

Materials
- 3 rectangles of mirror board or 3 mirrors 14 cm x 6 cm
- sticky tape
- card
- tracing paper
- coloured paper or sequins
- glue
- a sharp pencil

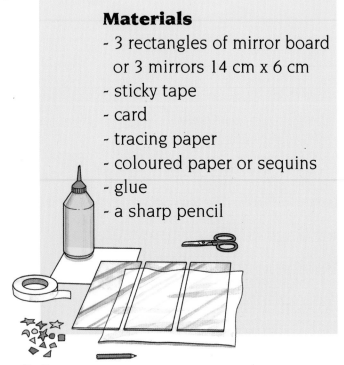

1. Tape the three rectangles of mirror board together, with the mirrors facing inwards to make a triangular prism (Figure 1).
2. On the card, draw around one end of the prism to make a triangle (Figure 2). Cut it out and make a hole in the centre with the tip of a sharp pencil.

3. On the tracing paper, draw two triangles in the same way. Draw flaps about 0.5 cm wide along each edge (Figure 3) and cut the triangles out.

4. Glue the flaps of the two triangles together along two sides only to make a little pocket (Figure 4).

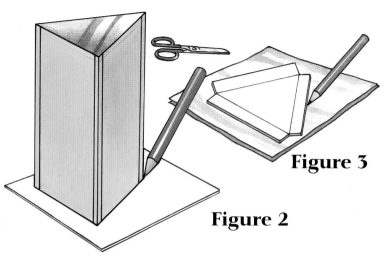

Figure 2

Figure 3

Figure 4

Figure 5

5. Fill the pocket with sequins or bits of coloured card (Figure 5).

6. Tape the pocket to one end of the prism (Figure 6) and the card triangle to the other. Hold the kaleidoscope to the light, look through the hole and turn it to change the patterns you see (Figure 7).

WHAT THIS SHOWS

Mirrors are made of smooth glass with shiny metal on the back. We see a reflection when light from an object bounces off the mirror into our eyes. Light from the sequins bounces between the mirrors and we see their reflections over and over again.

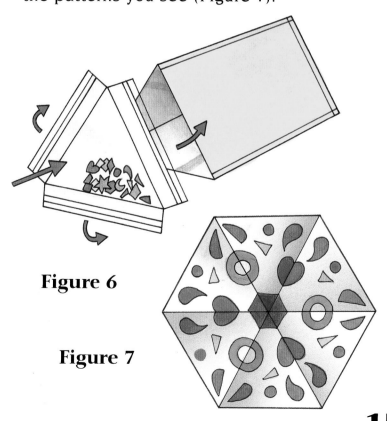

Figure 6

Figure 7

Reflection

Days are bright because sunlight is reflected and scattered in all directions by the Earth's atmosphere.

HOW LIGHT BOUNCES

Cut out a circle of foil large enough to cover the beam of a torch. Make a hole in it with a pencil (Figure 1). Cover the torch with the foil (Figure 2) to create a narrow beam of light. In a dark room, shine the torch onto a mirror. You will see a beam of light reflected off the mirror. Ask a friend to hold up a ball. Take aim and try to hit the ball with the beam of reflected light (Figure 3). Change the angle of the beam by moving the mirror or the torch (Figure 4).

Figure 1

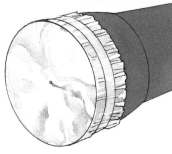

Figure 2

Figure 3

WHY IT WORKS

If you shine a beam of light straight at a smooth surface like a mirror, it will bounce straight back. If the light hits the surface at an angle, it will be reflected back at exactly the same angle. By looking at where the ball is in relation to you and the torch, you can calculate the angle you need to make the beam of light reflect onto the ball.

Figure 4

Fix a clear sheet of plastic upright in modelling clay. Put a small candle on one side of the plastic and light it. Angle your finger on the other side of the plastic so that it looks like the flame is coming from your finger.

HOW IT WORKS
Your friend sees the reflection of the candle flame on the shiny plastic, creating the illusion that your finger is on fire.

MIRROR WRITING

Write your name on a piece of paper and put it in front of a small mirror. Copy what you see in the mirror. Now put this writing in front of the mirror and you will see a reflection of your name. Mirror writing looks like secret code so you can use it for secret messages and use a mirror to decode it. Reflections in the mirror look the wrong way round because they bounce straight back off the mirror and your image is reversed. Your left hand looks like your right hand in the mirror.

Light is reflected in different ways. It bounces off smooth surfaces and it scatters when it hits rough surfaces. We see objects when this reflected light goes into our eyes.

17

Refraction

Light going through empty space with nothing in its way will travel in a straight line. But when light goes from air through something transparent such as glass or water, it is refracted, which means its direction changes. This happens because light travels at different speeds through different materials. When light passes through raindrops or a triangular shaped piece of glass called a prism, it is refracted and split into colours. Light is always on the move, it never stays still.

See light refract as it passes through water

METHOD NOTES
Use a jar or container with straight sides.

Materials
- a piece of card
- scissors
- a glass jar with a screw top
- a few drops of milk
- a torch

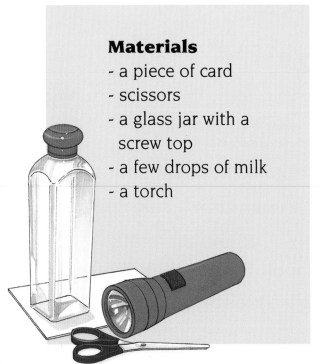

Figure 1

1 Cut a narrow slit in one end of the card (Figure 1) and bend the card so that it can stand up on its long side.

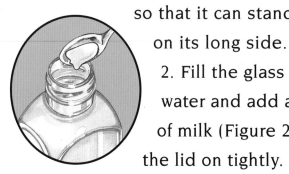

2. Fill the glass jar with water and add a few drops of milk (Figure 2). Screw the lid on tightly.

Figure 2

18

Figure 3

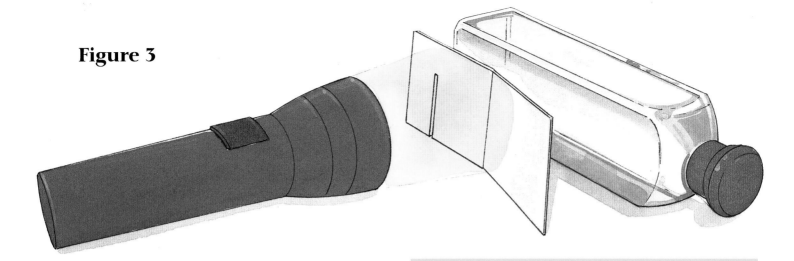

3. In a dark room, lie the jar on its side on a table.

4. Stand the card on the table next to the glass jar. Then shine the torch through the slit into the jar (Figure 3).

5. See the beam of light bend as it goes through the water and then bend the other way as it passes back into the air.

Half fill a clear plastic bag with water and hold it up to a window. What can you see through the bag? Can you see rainbow colours? Try and work out what happens to the light as it passes through the water.

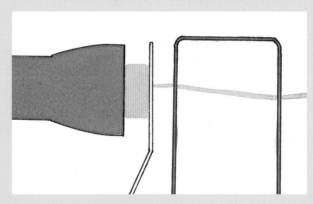

WHAT THIS SHOWS

Light travels faster through air than through glass or water. As it goes from the air into the water, it slows down and slightly changes direction.

This is called refraction. The beam of light bends as it enters the water. It travels in a straight line through the water and then changes direction again as it leaves the water and goes back into the air.

19

Refraction

SEE A BEAM OF LIGHT

Spread some newspaper on the floor in a dark room. Gently sprinkle flour through a sieve onto the paper. Get a friend to shine a torch through the flour to light up the grains and you will be able to see the path of the beam of light (Figure 1).

Figure 1

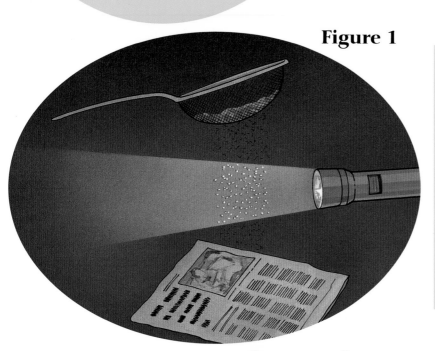

WHAT THIS SHOWS

When sunlight shines through dust or mist, when headlights shine through rain and when your torch shines through grains of flour, the drops of water and grains are lit up letting you see the straight path of the light rays.

Disappearing visions

Thirsty desert travellers think they see a pool of water (an oasis). What they really see is a mirage, a reflection of blue sky shimmering in hot air near the ground.

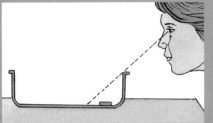

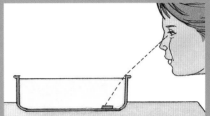

Put an empty bowl on a table and put a coin in the bottom. Fix it in place with modelling clay. Look at the coin and move backwards until the coin just disappears from view. Stay in the same position and get a friend to pour water into the bowl. Watch the coin reappear as if by magic!

WHY IT WORKS

The water bends the light from the coin and brings it back into view.

BENDING PENCILS

Half fill a glass of water and stand a pencil in it. If you look at the pencil through the side of the glass it seems to bend where it goes into the water. Light rays from the pencil bend as they leave the water making it look bent, although when you pull it out you will see that it is really still straight.

Light never stops moving in straight lines called rays. It travels at different speeds through air, water and glass. As it goes from one of these materials to another it changes direction or refracts.

Lenses

We cannot change what we see with our eyes, but we can use lenses in glasses, cameras, microscopes, binoculars and telescopes to make things look clearer, bigger or smaller. A concave lens curves inwards towards the middle and makes things look smaller. A convex lens bulges outwards towards the middle and makes things look bigger. In binoculars, convex lenses magnify what you see, making distant objects appear to be much closer than they are.

Make a microscope with a drop of water for a lens

METHOD NOTES
Ask an adult to cut the bottle with a craft knife for you.

Materials
- transparent plastic bottle
- a craft knife
- a small mirror
- modelling clay
- a drop of water
- scissors
- a hair
- a drinking straw

1. Cut the top off the bottle. Cut a narrow strip from two opposite sides of the bottle and keep them (Figure 1).
2. Cut two horizontal slits in the other two opposite sides, near the top. Push each end of one of the strips into the slits to make a platform (Figure 2).

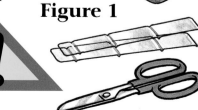

Figure 1

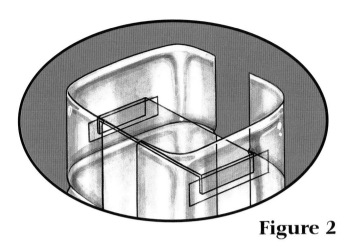

Figure 2

3. Prop the mirror at an angle on the modelling clay in the bottom of the bottle to reflect light upwards (Figure 3).

4. Dip a drinking straw in water and block the top hole with your finger. Take your finger off the straw to release one drop of water onto the platform.

5. Put the hair on the other strip and hold it under the drop of water. Look at it through the drop of water and see how it looks bigger (Figure 4).

Figure 3

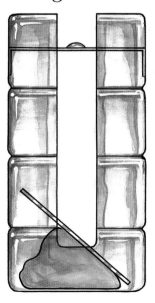

Look at other things – a tiny piece of newspaper with small print, a grain of sugar and a petal for example.

WHAT THIS SHOWS

The drop of water acts like a tiny convex lens (a). The mirror reflects light up onto the hair.

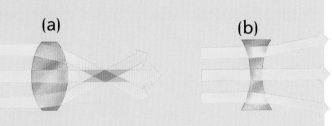

(a)   (b)

Light rays from the hair bend and converge – come closer together – as they pass through the drop of water and make the hair look bigger. Light rays bend and spread out as they pass through a concave lens (b), making things look smaller.

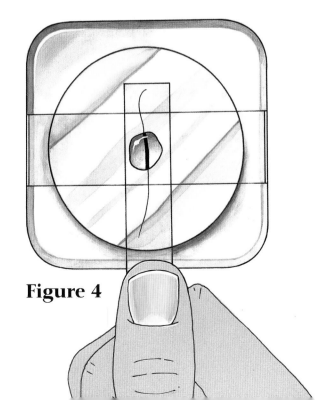

Figure 4

Lenses

CONCAVE AND CONVEX LENSES

Borrow a pair of glasses from someone with short sight to use as a concave lens. Use a magnifying glass as a convex lens. Cut a hole in a piece of card and bend the card so it stands up (Figure 1). Tape a comb over the hole (Figure 2). Put the magnifying glass in front of the hole (Figure 3). In a darkened room, shine a torch through the hole so that the rays shine on a book (Figure 3). See the rays created by the comb focus to a point. Replace the magnifying glass with the glasses and see the rays spread out (Figure 4).

Concave lenses in glasses help people with short sight and convex lenses help people with long sight to see clearly. Contact lenses work in the same way but are put straight onto the eye.

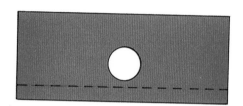

Figure 1

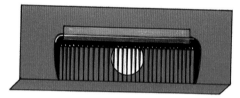

Figure 2

Figure 3

Figure 4

WHY IT WORKS
A convex lens bends the rays so that they focus, or come together, at a point making things look bigger. A concave lens bends the rays so that instead of focusing, they spread out and make things look smaller.

24

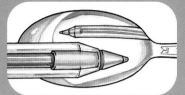

MAGNIFY THE MOON

A concave mirror, like a convex lens, magnifies objects. Put a concave make-up mirror in a window facing the Moon. Hold a flat mirror so that you can see the reflection of the Moon in the make-up mirror (Figure 1). Now look at that reflection through a magnifying glass to see a clear image. Mirrors and convex lenses are used in telescopes to look at the stars.

Figure 1

Figure 2

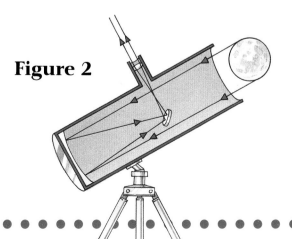

Concave and convex mirrors and lenses are used all around us every day to bend light and change the way we see things – from tiny creatures under a microscope to distant stars through a telescope.

25

Colours of light

Light we see from the Sun looks white so we call it white light. In fact, light is made up of hundreds of colours called the spectrum. People call the colours of the rainbow red, orange, yellow, green, blue, indigo and violet. White light splits into these colours when it passes through a triangular piece of glass called a prism. Sunlight splits when it passes through raindrops that act as tiny prisms and we see a rainbow.

Make a rainbow to see the seven colours of light

METHOD NOTES
You can use a torch or a beam of sunlight for this experiment.

Materials
- black card
- scissors
- a bowl of water
- a mirror
- modelling clay
- smaller piece of white card
- a torch

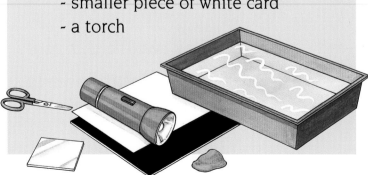

1. Cut a horizontal split just below the top edge of the black card (Figure 1).
2. Bend the bottom of the card so it can stand upright.
3. Half fill a glass bowl with water.

Figure 1

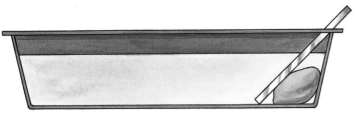

Figure 2

4. Angle a mirror so that it is half in and half out of the water (Figure 2). Use modelling clay to keep it in place.

5. Stand the black card with the white card in front of it, with the slit facing the mirror (Figure 3).

6. Shine the torch through the slit at the mirror (Figure 3). Adjust the mirror until you see a rainbow on the white card.

Figure 3

WHAT THIS SHOWS

A prism is created in the triangular shape between the mirror and the water. As the ray of light passes through the prism, each colour travels at a slightly different speed and bends at a different angle. The white light splits into a spectrum and you see a rainbow reflected onto the white card.

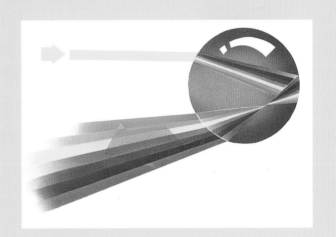

Are rainbows really round?
If you stood on a mountain and looked down on a rainbow, you would see that it is actually a whole circle. It usually looks like an arch because we can only see part of it from the ground.

Colours of light

MAKE RAINBOW COLOURS

Put a bowl of water in some bright sunshine and sprinkle in a few drops of oil. Stir the oil gently and see rainbow colours floating on the water.

Figure 1

Buy some bubble mixture or make your own by adding bubble bath to water. Blow bubbles outside on a sunny day and see rainbow colours on their skin (Figure 1). Light is reflected between the thin layers of the bubbles' soapy skin and between the thin layers of oil on the water. The light is split and a spectrum is created in the soapy and oily skins.

wavelength

DIFFERENT COLOURS

Each colour of light travels in tiny waves – all with a different wavelength. Waves are measured from the top of one wave to the next. Red has the longest wavelength and violet has the shortest.

WHY THE SKY IS RED AT SUNSET

Stir a teaspoon of milk into a jar of water (Figure 1). Shine a torch sideways through the jar. The milky water looks blue (Figure 1). Move the torch so that the light is shining through the jar towards you. The water now looks yellow (Figure 2). Stir in a little more milk and shine the torch again – the water now looks pink (Figure 3).

Figure 2

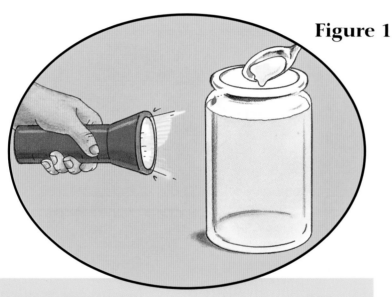

Figure 1

Figure 3

WHAT THIS SHOWS

The milky water looks blue as blue light is scattered out of the jar. Yellow light shone towards you still looks yellow as none of it is scattered. In the third case, only red light can get through the cloudier liquid. At sunset the low Sun travels through more particles in the atmosphere. Only red light gets through.

Sunlight splits into many colours. Tiny particles in the Earth's atmosphere scatter blue light, making the sky look blue in the day.

Mixing light

Light and colour go together, you can't have one without the other. We see when light enters our eyes. We see colour with light sensitive cells in our eyes, called cones, which detect the three primary colours of light – red, green and blue. The things around us look different colours because of the colour of light they reflect. A green leaf for example reflects green light into our eyes and absorbs, or takes in, all the other colours.

Mix the primary colours of light

METHOD NOTES
This experiment works best if you do it with two friends.

Materials
- red, blue and green cellophane
- scissors
- 3 cardboard tubes
- 3 torches
- sticky tape
- white card

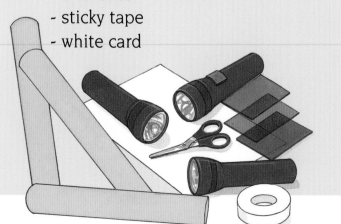

1. Cut out a circle of each colour of cellophane to make three filters. Ensure that the circles are bigger than the end of the tubes (Figure 1).

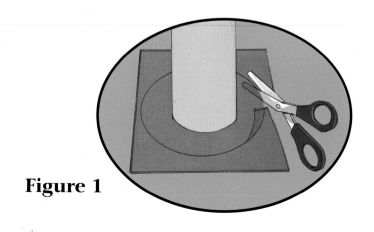

Figure 1

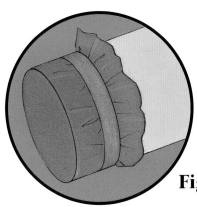

2. Tape a coloured filter to the end of each tube (Figure 2).

Figure 2

3. Put the white card on the floor. You and two friends need a torch and a tube each.

4. In a darkened room, shine torches down each of the tubes to make three pools of coloured light on the white card (Figure 3).

5. Move the lights around so they overlap and make new colours (Figure 3). Can you see a pool of white light where the three colours overlap?

Figure 3

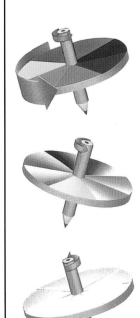

Why not try making a colour wheel? Cut out a circle of card. Paint the seven colours of the rainbow in order on the card. Push a pencil through the middle and spin the wheel. The colours mix and make white light.

WHAT THIS SHOWS

You have seen how light can be split into many colours. When all the colours are mixed together again, they make white light. Mixing two coloured lights together makes new colours. Green and blue light make a pale blue light called cyan. Blue and red light make a pink light called magenta. Green and red light make yellow light. Coloured filters on spotlights are used to create coloured lighting effects on stage.

Mixing light

LOOK AT OBJECTS IN COLOURED LIGHT

Cut a big hole in the lid of a shoe box (Figure 1). Cut out a small hole in one of the short sides of the box (Figure 2). Put different coloured things such as a banana, a tomato and a green apple in the box. Lie a sheet of red cellophane over the lid.

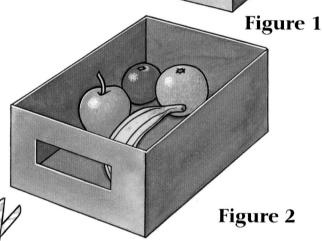

Figure 1

Shine a torch through the filter and look through the hole in the side of the box and see how the red filter changes the colours of the fruit in the box (Figure 3). Red objects in the box look pale and green ones are dark. Try using different coloured filters.

Figure 2

Figure 3

WHAT THIS SHOWS

A red filter only allows red light through, just as a green filter only lets green light through, and so on. Green objects look dark through the red filter because they absorb red light, They can't reflect green light because no green light comes through the filter.

A blue banana!
Some animals' eyes are able to see more colours than ours. Very often these animals are brightly coloured themselves. They use these colours for display and defence.

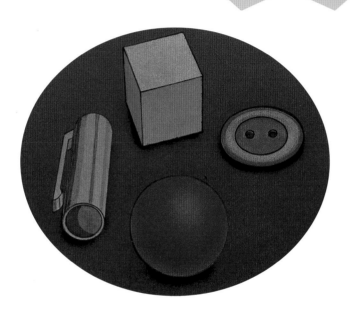

SEEING IN THE DARK

Look at a collection of coloured objects in a darkened room, with just enough light to see by. Can you tell what colours they are? There is not enough light for your eyes to detect different colours. We see what little light there is with cells in our eyes called rods, which detect only black and white.

TWILIGHT

Look out of the window at twilight – when the sun has just sunk below the horizon. See how colours begin to fade as the light disappears.

White light can be split into the colours of the spectrum. Coloured light can be mixed to make white light. Human and animal eyes are adapted to see colour and light in different ways.

Colours and dyes

Plants, soil, rocks and animals have natural colours called pigments. These materials can be ground into coloured powders and used to make paints and dyes. Natural and chemical pigments used in paints and dyes can make an enormous range of different shades of every colour which we use to paint and dye the things we make. Pigments in these coloured objects reflect some of the colours of light into our eyes and we see those colours.

Tie–dye cloth in a natural pigment

METHOD NOTES
You must wear an apron and rubber gloves for this project.

Materials
- chopping board
- knife
- beetroot
- saucepan
- tongs or long-handled spoon
- white cotton material
- string
- scissors

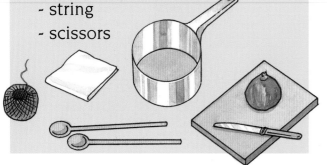

Figure 2

Figure 1

1. On a chopping board, carefully cut a beetroot into small cubes (Figure 1).
2. Put the cubes into a pan of water, bring it to the boil and simmer for about 15 minutes until the water turns purple (Figure 2).

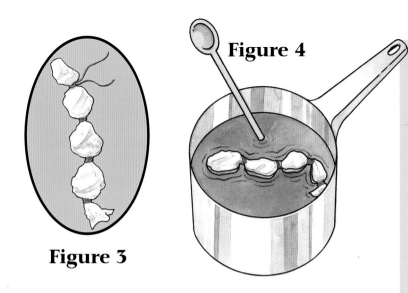

Figure 4

Figure 3

WHY IT WORKS

Vegetables contain coloured pigments which are released into the boiling water. Beetroot, red cabbage and cherries contain red pigment. Spinach contains green pigment and onion skins contain yellow pigment. Soaking the material in the coloured water dyes it. The dye cannot reach the parts of the cloth you tie tightly with string, so they stay white. Experiment with tying the string to make different patterns on the cloth.

3. Take the pan off the heat and leave the water to cool.

4. Roll up the material and tie string around it tightly in three or four different places (Figure 3).

5. Drop the material in the purple water and leave it for a few minutes (Figure 4).

6. Take it out with tongs or a draining spoon (Figure 5), cut the string (Figure 6) and hang it up to dry (Figure 7).

Figure 7

Figure 5

Figure 6

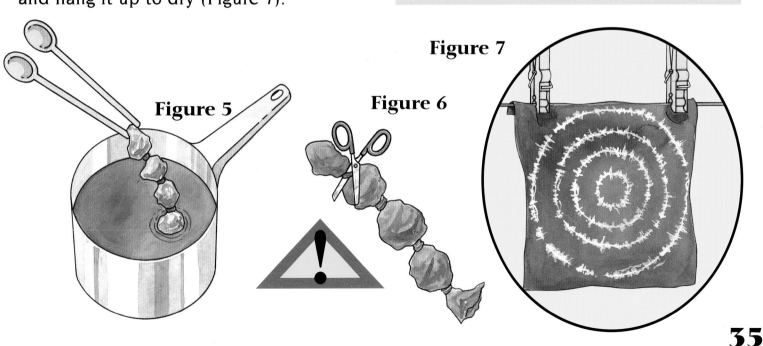

Colours and dyes

Shades of colour are made by mixing pigments, or dyes, together to make new colours. Mixing pigments has a different effect from mixing coloured light.

SPLITTING COLOURS

Several different pigments are used to make the inks in coloured pens. Cut circles out of kitchen towel (Figure 1). Draw a blob of colour in the middle of each one with non-waterproof felt-tip pens (Figure 1).

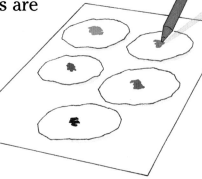

Figure 1

Put a drinking straw in water and cover the top with your finger (Figure 2). Take your finger off to release a drop of water onto each blob of colour (Figure 3). Watch the colour spread out and see new colours appear (Figure 4).

Figure 2

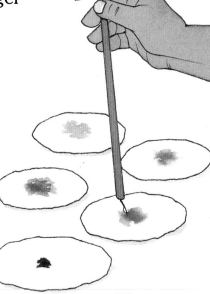

WHAT THIS SHOWS

The water travels through the absorbent kitchen towel and spreads the pigments in the ink. It spreads each pigment at a slightly different speed. This lets you see all the separate pigments that make up each coloured ink.

Figure 3

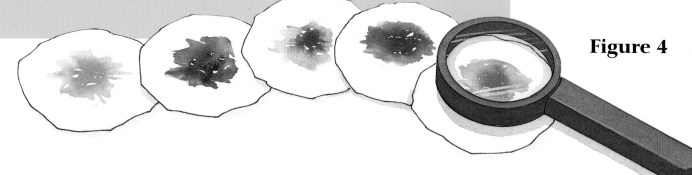

Figure 4

Beetle juice

Cochineal is a bright red dye made from grinding small red beetles. It is used as a food dye so you have probably eaten it.

THE AMAZING MAGIC DOTS
Use dots to create a whole picture

Draw a picture just using dots of colour. Use blue and yellow dots together where you want green, yellow and red dots for orange, and blue and red for purple. Stand back and see the colours and shapes appear.

WHY IT WORKS

Your brain mixes the coloured dots for you and you see the new colours.

COLOUR WHEEL

Make a colour wheel like this. Start with the primary colours of paint – red, yellow and blue. Mix them to make the secondary colours – orange, green and purple. When you put opposite colours on the wheel next to each other, they can look much brighter.

Colours reflected from pigments are different from the colours of the spectrum. We see colours when pigments reflect certain colours of light into our eyes.

Taking pictures

Every day we see still and moving images from all over the world in newspapers and on television, captured by cameras on film and video and with digital technology. We have family photograph albums and home movies. X-ray cameras take pictures of bones inside our bodies and infra-red cameras take pictures of the light we can't normally see. Our eyes work like a small and very precise camera letting us see the world around us.

Make a pinhole camera

METHOD NOTES
The brighter the object you choose, the better the image will be in your camera.

Materials
- sticky tape
- tracing paper
- a small square box
- a pin
- dark towel
- magnifying glass

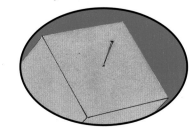

Figure 1   **Figure 2**

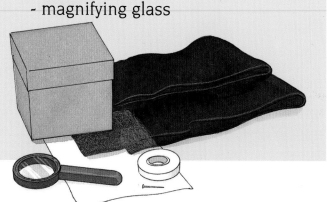

1. Tape tracing paper smoothly over the open side of the box (Figure 1).
2. Make a pinhole in the middle of the side of the box opposite the tracing paper (Figure 2).

Figure 3

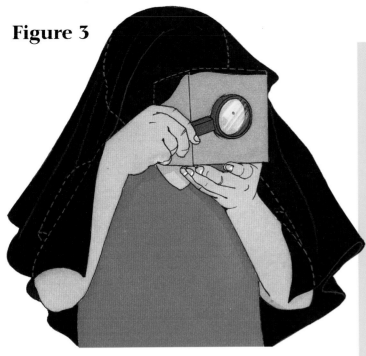

3. Put the towel over your head and the box to block out the light (Figure 3).
4. Point the pinhole at something very bright and look at the tracing paper.
5. Hold a magnifying glass between the pinhole and the object you are looking at for a clearer, bigger image.
6. You will see an upside-down image of the bright object reflected onto the tracing paper (Figure 4).

Figure 4

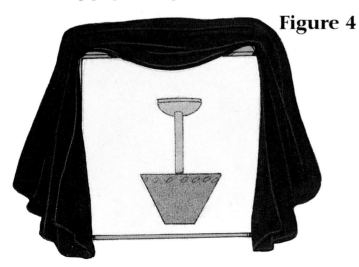

WHY IT WORKS

Light rays travel in straight lines. Rays from the top and bottom of the object cross over as they pass through the pinhole and reverse the image onto the tracing paper, so you see it upside down. In a camera, the image is projected onto photographic film containing chemicals that preserve it as a photograph.

Your eyes work in the same way. A lens at the front of your eye focuses light onto light sensitive cells in the retina at the back of your eye. An upside-down image is sent to the brain, which turns it around again.

Our eyes are only designed to see a small amount of light called visible light. Cameras can be designed to capture light that is invisible to the human eye.

Taking pictures

HOW X-RAYS WORK

X-rays can travel through soft things like skin or clothes. They are used to check inside luggage at airports and in hospitals to see broken bones. Draw around your hand on some white card and cut it out (Figure 1). Stick the silhouette of your hand between two sheets of white paper (Figure 2). Look at the paper – you can't see the hand (Figure 3). Hold the paper up and shine a bright light behind it. You can see the outline of the hand clearly now (Figure 4).

Figure 1

Figure 2

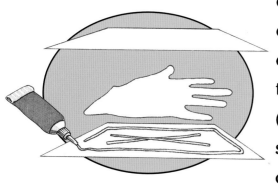

Figure 3

Figure 4

WHY IT WORKS

Visible light is a small part of the electromagnetic spectrum. Gamma rays, X-rays, ultraviolet rays, visible light rays, infra-red rays, microwaves and radio waves are all electromagnetic waves with different wavelengths. X-rays have a much shorter wavelength than visible light rays. X-ray light goes through our skin but not our bones and we see shadows of our bones.

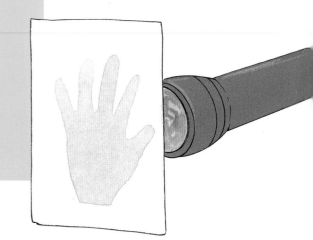

THE AMAZING FISH IN A BOWL
See how light can trick your eyes

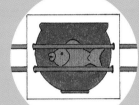

You need a piece of thick card 6 x 6 cm with two holes on opposite edges. Loop 60 cm of string through the holes. Draw a fish on one side of the card and a bowl on the other. Twist the string round and round and then pull each end so that the card spins rapidly.

WHY IT WORKS

The fish appears to be in the bowl. Because the two pictures move so quickly, your eyes see them as one picture.

Hot cat

Infra-red cameras capture invisible light called infra-red radiation, which is given out by anything hot. They can take pictures of things that would usually be invisible at night.

MAKE A FLICK BOOK

Cartoons are made from sequences of pictures moving so quickly that our brain sees them as moving film. Draw a sequence of pictures of a figure running along. Staple the pictures together and flick the pages rapidly. You will see your figure running.

Cameras

focus light through lenses to capture images on film in the same way as lenses in our eyes focus light onto light sensitive cells at the back of our eyes.

41

Weird light

The Sun, lamps, torches and candles are familiar luminous objects that give out light. Light also comes from other, stranger sources. You can see flashes of light caused by static electricity when you take off a nylon shirt; fireflies flash out light signals at night; fluorescent strips shine in the glare of headlights; and chemicals glow inside light sticks. Lasers control and use the power of light, and light travels along fibre optic cables carrying information.

Make light bend and pour to see how fibre optics work

METHOD NOTES
Make the pin hole and the clear patch about one third of the way up from the bottom of the bottle.

Materials
- scissors
- a clear plastic bottle
- black paint
- a torch
- a pin
- a large glass bowl

Figure 1

1. Cut the top off the plastic bottle (Figure 1).
2. Paint the outside black leaving a small, clear patch on one side (Figure 2).
3. Using a pin, make a small hole in the other side of the bottle, opposite the clear patch (Figure 2).

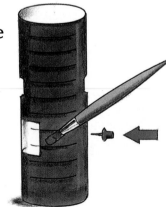

Figure 2

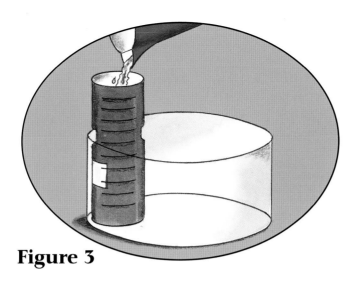

Figure 3

4. In a dark room, stand the bottle on one side of the bowl, with the clear patch facing out and the hole facing in (Figure 3).

5. Fill the bottle with water (Figure 3). Then shine light at the clear patch.

6. Pressure will push the water through the hole in a thin stream which will glow brightly with the light from the torch (Figure 4).

Figure 4

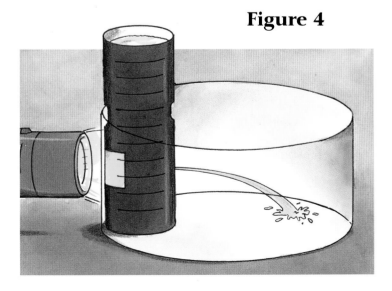

WHAT THIS SHOWS

Light carries information such as telephone and television signals along glass wires called fibre optic cables. The cables channel light fast and efficiently around bends and over long distances. The stream of water acts like a fibre optic wire. Light rays bounce off the sides of the stream and are reflected inside it, making it glow.

Fibre optic cables carry light along their path by reflecting it back and forth off the sides of their thin cables.

Weird light

MAKE LIGHT WITH SUGAR CUBES

Grains of sugar are tiny crystals. Sugar lumps are made by packing grains of sugar together in cubes. Put some sugar lumps in a transparent plastic food bag and tie the top (Figure 1). Put the bag on a chopping board and darken the room. Bash the bag with a wooden rolling pin and you will see sparks of light coming from the crystals of sugar (Figure 2).

Figure 1

Figure 2

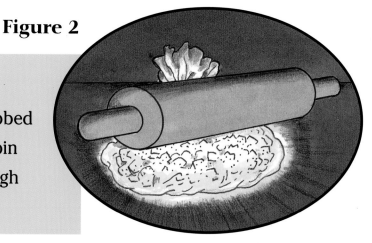

WHY IT WORKS

Light is produced when the crystals are rubbed together. Hitting the sugar with the rolling pin rubs the grains of sugar together with enough force to produce sparks of light.

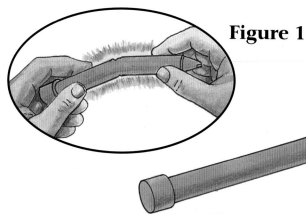

Figure 1

Figure 2

DISCOVER WHY PARTY STICKS GLOW

There are two different chemicals in a party glow stick, one in an inner and one in an outer tube. When you snap the tube (Figure 1), the chemicals mix and glow. You can stop the reaction between the chemicals (Figure 2) by putting it in a freezer. To restart the reaction and make it glow again, dip it in warm water.

Worms that glow

Glow worms are like party glow sticks glowing in the dark. Chemicals in their bodies mix to make a greenish light. They can turn the light on and off any time they choose.

PAINT PICTURES THAT GLOW

Luminous paint works by storing light. When it becomes dim, you can recharge it by leaving it in bright light again. Paint two pictures, one with luminous and one with ordinary paint or pens. Put the pictures in shade or dull light and you will see how luminous paint glows with stored light.

Many different kinds of light illuminate the world. The Sun is the Earth's main source of light. Without light and heat from the Sun, there would be no life on Earth.

Glossary

Concave lens
A curved piece of glass that spreads out light rays. It makes things appear smaller.

Convex lens
A curved piece of glass that brings light rays together. It makes things appear larger.

Fibre optic cable
A very thin piece of glass along which light can travel long distances, carrying huge amounts of information such as telephone, television and internet signals.

Light ray
A narrow beam of light.

Microscope
An arrangement of lenses and mirrors that can magnify things invisible to the naked eye.

Opaque
The description of a material such as a brick through which no light can pass.

Pigments
Substances that give paints and dyes their colour.

Primary colours
Colours that can be combined to make all other colours. The primary colours of light are red, green and blue. The primary colours of paints are red, yellow and blue.

Prism
A transparent wedge of glass that refracts (changes the direction of) light, splitting it into all the colours of the rainbow.

Reflection
The way light bounces off a surface. It reflects off a flat surface at the same angle as it hits the surface.

Refraction

The way light changes direction when it passes from one material (such as air) to another (such as water).

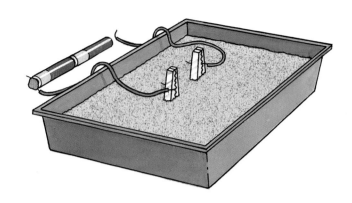

Shadow

A dark area formed on a surface, which takes the shape of an object that has blocked light rays from the Sun or another light source.

Spectrum

All the colours of visible light, from those with the shortest wavelength (violet) to those with the longest (red).

Telescope

A scientific instrument that uses lenses and mirrors to magnify far away objects such as stars and galaxies in the night sky.

Translucent

The description of a material such as tracing paper that lets some light pass through.

Transparent

The description of a material such as glass that lets all or nearly all light pass through it.

Wavelength

Light travels in waves. A wavelength is the distance from the top of one light wave to the top of the next. We see lights of different wavelengths as different colours.

X-rays

A kind of wave that cannot be seen by the human eye. X-rays pass through some materials that are opaque to visible light.

Index

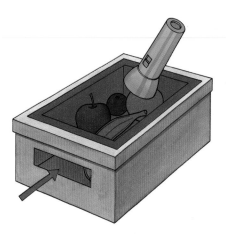